THIS CANDLEWICK BOOK BELONGS TO:

Second U.S. paperback edition 2001

The Library of Congress has cataloged the hardcover edition as follows:

King-Smith, Dick.
I love guinea pigs / by Dick King-Smith;
illustrated by Anita Jeram. — 1st U.S. ed.
(Read and wonder books)
ISBN 1-56402-389-3 (hardcover)
1. Guinea pigs as pets—Juvenile literature. [1. Guinea pigs.
2. Pets.] I. Jeram, Anita, ill. II. Title. III. Series:
Read and wonder.
SF459.G9K55   1995
636'.93234—dc20   94-4880
ISBN 0-7636-0150-0 (paperback 1st ed.)
ISBN 0-7636-1435-1 ((paperback 2nd ed.)

10 9 8 7 6 5 4

Printed in China

This book was typeset in New Baskerville.
The illustrations were done in line and watercolor.

Candlewick Press
2067 Massachusetts Avenue
Cambridge, Massachusetts 02140

visit us at www.candlewick.com

I LOVE GUINEA PIGS

Dick King-Smith

illustrated by

Anita Jeram

CANDLEWICK PRESS
CAMBRIDGE, MASSACHUSETTS

There's a silly old saying that
if you hold a guinea pig up
by its tail, its eyes
will drop out.

Well of course they wouldn't,

even if you could—which you couldn't,

because guinea pigs don't have tails.

What do guinea pigs
have in common with pigs?

The males and females are
known as boars and sows.

And they aren't pigs either.

They're rodents—like mice and rats
and squirrels.

Rodents have special front teeth
that are great for gnawing things.
These teeth go on growing throughout
the animal's life and are self-sharpening.

As for the other part of their name, guinea pigs were first brought to Europe about four hundred years ago by Spanish sailors, probably from a country in South America called Dutch Guiana. And the sailors called them "guiana pigs."

In fact, the guinea pig is a member
of the cavy family, and its
Latin name is *Cavia porcellus*
(which means a piggy-looking cavy).

Anyway, whatever they're called,

it's the way they look that I've

always liked. They're so

chunky and chubby

and cuddly, with their blunt

heads and sturdy bodies and short legs.

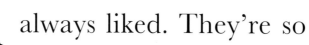

smooth

Peruvian

They come in tons of different colors, and
they can be smooth-coated or rough-coated
or long-coated, not to mention
the other varieties.
I've had hundreds of
guinea pigs over the last fifty years,
but I've always liked the Abyssinians best.

crested

sheltie

Abyssinians

Guinea pigs are such sensible animals.

They're awfully easy to keep,

because they aren't fussy.

They don't like the cold, of course, or the damp, any more than you would, and they're not happy living in a poky little place, any more than you would be. But as long as they have a comfortable, warm, dry place to live, guinea pigs are as happy as can be.

Guinea pigs like a really big roomy hutch or, better still, a wire pen out on the grass.

They're hardy animals and don't often get sick. Properly cared for, they can live a long time.

Most guinea pigs live for about five to eight years.

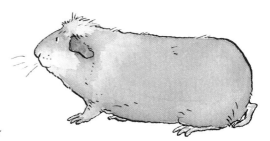

I once had a crested sow
named Zen. She lived two years
with me and then eight more
with one of my daughters.
People's hair grows whiter
as they age, but Zen's
grew darker.

Guinea pigs need
plenty of food.

They love eating, just like you do, and feeding
them is half the fun of having them.

Some people, of course, feed them
nothing but hay and pellets from
the pet store, and they're just fine.

But how boring a diet like that must
be, both for the piggy-looking
cavy and its
owner.

I always used to give my
guinea pigs lots of other kinds of
food as well: cabbage and cauliflower leaves,
carrots, pieces of bread and apple peelings, and
wild plants, like dandelions
and clover. I gave them
water, too, of course.
Guinea pigs need
clean drinking
water every day. And their water
bottle often needs washing,
because they like blowing pieces
of food back up the spout.

One especially nice thing
about guinea pigs is that
if you handle them
regularly, and carry them around, stroke
them, talk to them, and make a fuss
over them, they become
really fond of you.

The correct way to pick up
a guinea pig is with one hand
over its shoulders and the other
supporting its bottom.

Another nice thing about guinea pigs is that they talk a lot.

When they want food or water, they often give a sort of whistle, sometimes low, sometimes loud.

Boars say *chutter* when they're squaring up for a fight.

So do sows when their babies pester them too much.

Other things guinea pigs say are

putt

chut

tweet

and *drr.*

But when one guinea pig says *purr* to another
guinea pig, it's as plain as the nose on your face
that it only means one thing:

"I love you."

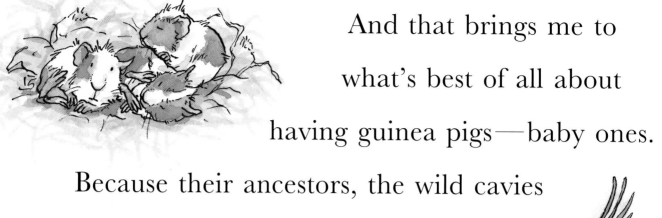

And that brings me to
what's best of all about
having guinea pigs—baby ones.
Because their ancestors, the wild cavies
of South America, lived out in the
open with enemies all around them,
their young ones had to be
ready to run for it.

So the guinea pig sow carries
her unborn litter for a very
long time, about seventy days,

and they arrive in

the world fully furred, with their

eyes open and their mouths already

filled with teeth.

Newborn guinea pigs
are such a comical sight.

Their heads and feet look too big for their bodies.

Baby rabbits are born blind and naked and helpless, but not baby guinea pigs.

But almost immediately

they show an interest in those two

favorite guinea pig pursuits—

eating

and conversation.

Of all the guinea pigs I've had,
there were two that I will never
forget. Both were Abyssinians,
both were boars, and each in his
time fathered dozens of lovely
big-headed, big-footed babies.

One was a bright golden color,
and his name was King Arthur.
The other was a blue roan named
Beach Boy. Both are buried in
my yard.

There's a solitary apple tree at the edge
of my lawn, and I like to look at it and think
that under it Beach Boy and King Arthur
lie peacefully, one on one side of the tree,
one on the other.

I'm not sad about this—
just happy to remember
what a lot of pleasure
I've had from all
my guinea pigs.

One especially nice
thing about guinea pigs
is that if you make a fuss
over them, they become
really fond of you.

DICK KING-SMITH is the author of *All Pigs Are Beautiful,* which *Booklist* called "as beguiling an introduction to pigs as any child could hope to see." He wrote *I Love Guinea Pigs* because "I've always had a soft spot for them. I started keeping them when I was six and only stopped, with great regret, when I was sixty." He recalls entering one of his guinea pigs in a guinea pig show, where it won third prize. "There were, however, only two other guinea pigs entered," he admits. The author of *Babe: The Gallant Pig,* Dick King-Smith has also written the delightful and popular Sophie series, *Lady Lollipop,* and *Dick King-Smith's Animal Friends.*

ANITA JERAM also illustrated Dick King-Smith's *All Pigs Are Beautiful* and notes, "One of the things pigs and guinea pigs have in common is their love for food. And like pigs, guinea pigs at first glance don't appear to act differently from one another. But when you get to know them, you see that they are all individuals." The author and illustrator of *Bunny, My Honey; Daisy Dare;* and *All Together Now,* Anita Jeram is also the illustrator of *Kiss Good Night* by Amy Hest and *Guess How Much I Love You* by Sam McBratney.